And let Your fire consume me

Breathe life oh breathe life into me

And let Your fire consume me

You built a bridge

That reached from heaven down to me

Though I'm unworthy

Once a captive now I'm free

CINDY MORGAN

CHRIS RODRIGUEZ

You raised the mountains up

To reach and touch the sky

You forged the depth of pain

And crossed the river wide

Before You Begin...

Look. I mean really *look*. Then, think.

It's the most important thing I do as an artist. If I want to paint, let's say, a vase of pink roses, I simply must have fresh, flouncy blooms sitting right next to my art easel. Then long before I pick up a pink pastel pencil to begin sketching, I'll sit back to take in the entire arrangement, lingering over it for a good half hour, looking at it from this way, then that. After observing the roses from every angle, I'll pull up close to examine the specifics: admiring the folds on the petals, the way the veins glow darker and brighter near the base, and how the thorns almost trace an invisible spiral up the stem.

I'll look at the roses for many hours before I paint them. And I'll think. Yes, about which oils to mix and brushes to use, but mainly I'll think about the One who created the roses in the first place. *God did this. He thought of this color, this fragrance. Truly, the rose is the Lord's and the fullness thereof!* When I ponder this and more, I can't help but become inspired. And when an artist is inspired, watch out! Oils can't get squeezed out of tubes fast enough, swirling and splattering and creating perhaps the happiest, most stunning painting of roses you've ever seen.

It's all about inspiration. And it all begins with looking and thinking.

It's an art a true aesthetic discipline that's been left in the dust of our jet-propelled culture. We zoom down the freeway, hardly noticing the sunset behind the billboard; or if we do walk, the pedometer on our wrist gets more attention than the delicate morning glories along the sidewalk. Somehow, someway, we must reclaim the art of *looking* and *thinking*.

The Hand That Paints the Sky provides just the inspiration. First, sit back and take in the entire book for long, lingering moments, flipping this way, then that. Then, get closer and delight in the specifics. Don't hurry, but ponder the breath-taking images of sunsets and mountains, the delicate photos of tiny leaves and tinier creatures, and most of all, the soul-stirring scriptures and quotes about the One who created the sunsets and mountains, leaves and creatures in the first place. When you do, you can't help but be inspired. And inspiration always means a fresh inhaling of the grace and exquisite loveliness of our Lord.

As an artist, may I encourage you to take not just a moment, but many long moments of refreshment and inspiration with this beautiful and elegant work you hold in your hands. You'll be inspired. And you, too, just might show the world how to look... think... and delight in the Hand that paints the sky.

JONI EARECKSON TADA

Summer 2003

The HAND *That* PAINTS *the* Sky

Copyright 2003 by New Leaf Press

Published by New Leaf Press, Green Forest, Arkansas, U.S.A.

Unless otherwise indicated, all Scripture quotations in this book are from the Holy Bible, the
New International Version, copyright 1973, 1978, 1984 by International Bible Society. All rights
reserved. Used by permission of Zondervan Bible Publishers, Grand Rapids, Michigan.

Editorial content, design, and production by Left Coast Design, Inc.

Portland, Oregon, U.S.A.

ISBN: 0-89221-554-2

Library of Congress: 2003106239

Printed and bound in the United States of America · Second Printing

www.newleafpress.net   www.lcoast.com

The HAND *That* PAINTS *the* Sky

NEW LEAF PRESS www.newleafpress.net

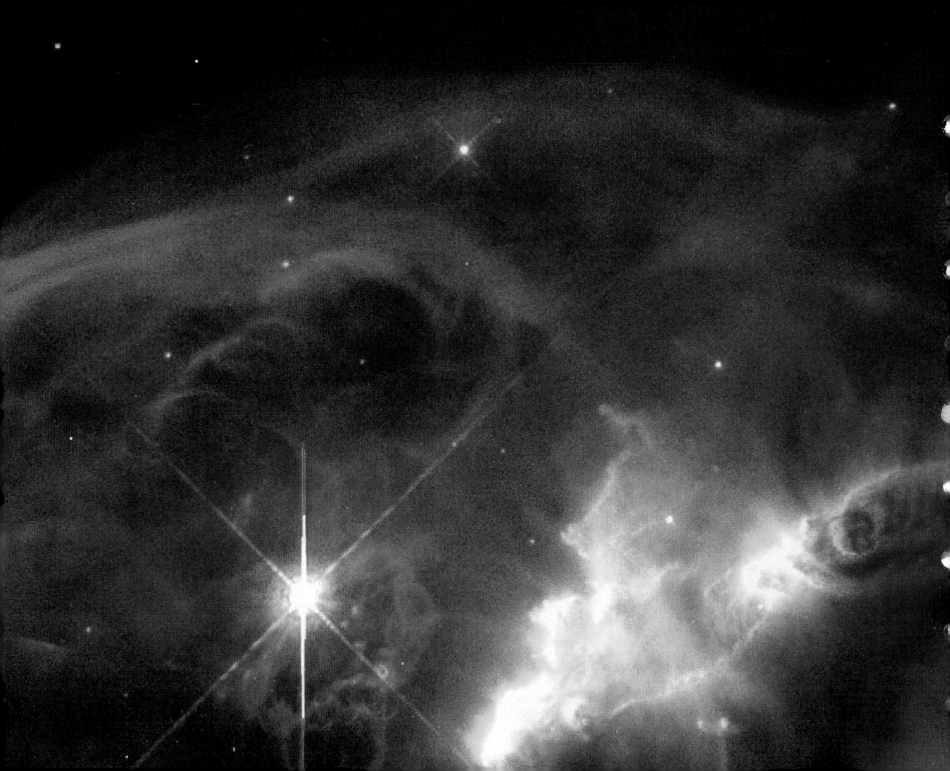

In the BEGINNING...

God created the heavens and the earth.

THE EARTH TAKES SHAPE LIKE CLAY
UNDER A SEAL; ITS FEATURES STAND
OUT LIKE THOSE OF A GARMENT.

JOB 38:14

The artist must create a spark before he can
make a fire and before art is born, the artist
must be ready to be consumed by the fire of his
own creation.

AUGUSTE RODIN

And God said, "Let there be light,"
and there was light.

It is the very nature of creation that the whole

world is like a burning bush — even though we

walk around all the time with our shoes on.

Seerveld
Rainbows for a Fallen World

The universe was made by God, it conformed to His nature, reflected His image and therefore was pronounced "good."

NED BUSTARD
It was Good . . . Making Art to the Glory of God

Some can write a sonnet

To describe in silvery words

The rising and the setting of the sun

Some can paint a picture

In shades of vibrant color

It almost looks like heaven when they're done

Lord, when I try to speak from my heart

I don't know where to start

When it comes to you I'm speechless

AVALON
In a Different Light, I'm Speechless

I applied streaks and blobs of colours onto the canvas with a palette knife and I made them sing with all the intensity I could. . .

WASSILY KANDINSKY

The emotions are sometimes so strong...

The strokes come like speech.

VINCENT VAN GOGH

The SECOND DAY...

And God said, "Let there be an expanse between the waters to separate water from water."

So God made the expanse and separated the water under the expanse from the water above it.

Yes, nature is personal to me. And did you know that nature even has its own personal scripture verse? Romans 8:19 tells us that "The creation waits in eager expectation for the sons of God to be revealed." The J.B. Phillips Translation renders it like this: "The whole creation is on tiptoe to see the wonderful sight of the sons of God coming into their own."

JONI EARECKSON TADA

Inspiration is God's breath taken into ourselves. God wants to breathe His creative life into us through the inspiration of the Holy Spirit.

JANICE ELSHEIMER
The Creative Call

FOR GREAT IS YOUR LOVE, HIGHER THAN
THE HEAVENS; YOUR FAITHFULNESS REACHES
TO THE SKIES.

PSALM 108:4

He wraps himself in light as with a garment; he stretches out the heavens like a tent and lays the beams of his upper chambers on their waves.

Psalm 104:2,3

God called the expanse "sky."

You do not know how paralyzing that staring of a blank canvas is; it says to the painter, You can't do anything. . . . Many painters are afraid of the blank canvas, but the blank canvas is afraid of the really passionate painter who is daring — and who has once and for all broken that spell of "you cannot".

VINCENT VAN GOGH

Blue skies expanse, stretched out before you

Puffs of white wrapped in trillium hue,

A place to fly kites, to dream and to dance

To run under barefoot when there is a chance.

You formed the sky with the wave of your hand

Placed over mountains, the seas and dry land,

You brushed it with color and transparent shades

Of pigments so fragile, translucently laid.

We lie on the grass and look up to the sky

We stare at its splendor through half opened eyes,

Did you paint with your fingers or in one single stroke?

Did you know all the magic and dreams you'd evoke?

KATHY VICK

HE MARKS OUT THE HORIZON ON
THE FACE OF THE WATERS FOR A
BOUNDARY BETWEEN LIGHT AND
DARKNESS.

JOB 26:10

And there was evening, and
there was morning.

*Color and light are two fundamental aspects
of painting and photography — unendingly
symbolic and powerful. These visual
dimensions, in which we are constantly
surrounded, remain a mystery to me. I
find myself constantly intrigued by the
influence of one upon the other.*

PATRICK ENDRES

Art is not what you see, but what you make others see.

EDGAR DEGAS

Blessed are they who see beautiful things in humble places where other people see nothing.

CAMILLE PISSARRO

Morning has broken like the first morning
Blackbird has spoken like the first bird
Praise for the singing, praise for the morning!
Praise for them springing fresh from the Word

Sweet the rain's new fall, sunlit from heaven
Like the first dew fall on the first grass
Praise for the sweetness of the wet garden
God's creation of the new day

ELEANOR FARJEON

I try to apply colors like words that shape poems, like notes that shape music.

JOAN MIRO

Lord, grant that I may always desire more than I can accomplish.

MICHELANGELO

I myself do nothing. The Holy Spirit accomplishes all through me.

WILLIAM BLAKE

THE PATH OF THE RIGHTEOUS IS LIKE THE FIRST GLEAM OF DAWN, SHINING EVER BRIGHTER TILL THE FULL LIGHT OF DAY.

PROVERBS 4:18

THE DAY IS YOURS, AND
YOURS ALSO THE NIGHT;
YOU ESTABLISHED THE SUN
AND MOON.

PSALM 74:16

THE SUN RISES AT ONE END OF
THE HEAVENS AND FOLLOWS
ITS COURSE TO THE OTHER END.
NOTHING CAN HIDE FROM
ITS HEAT.

PSALM 19:6

Now I really feel the landscape, I can be bold and include every tone of blue and pink: it's enchanting, it's delicious.   CLAUDE MONET

Creativity takes courage.

HENRI MATISSE

The THIRD DAY...

God said, "Let the water under the sky be gathered to one place, and let dry ground appear."

Art, like prayer, is really more about our giving to God than our performing for God. To delight in God — to focus solely on His pleasure — is to worship Him. And to worship is the true vocation of the artist's soul.

J. SAWYER
The Art of the Soul: Meditations for the Creative Spirit

God called the dry ground
"land," and the gathered
waters He called "seas."

*I know that to paint the sea really well, you
need to look at it every hour of every day in
the same place so that you can understand its
way in that particular spot; and that is why I
am working on the same motifs over and over
again, four or six times even.*

CLAUDE MONET

WHO SHUT UP THE SEA BEHIND
DOORS WHEN IT BURST FORTH
FROM THE WOMB, WHEN I MADE
THE CLOUDS ITS GARMENT AND
WRAPPED IT IN THICK DARKNESS,
WHEN I FIXED LIMITS FOR IT AND
SET ITS DOORS AND BARS IN PLACE,
WHEN I SAID, "THIS FAR YOU MAY
COME AND NO FARTHER; HERE IS
WHERE YOUR PROUD WAVES HALT"?

JOB 38:8-11

HE MAKES SPRINGS POUR WATER
INTO THE RAVINES; IT FLOWS
BETWEEN THE MOUNTAINS.

PSALM 104:10

These landscapes of water and reflection have become an obsession.

MONET

As water reflects a face,

so a man's heart reflects

the man.

PROVERBS 27:19

The mind of the painter should be like

a mirror which always takes the color

of the thing that it reflects, and which is

filled by as many images as there are

things placed before it.

LEONARDO DA VINCI

The big artist . . . keeps an eye on nature
and steals her tools.

THOMAS EAKINS

Great art picks up where nature ends.

MARC CHAGALL

All finite things reveal infinitude:

The mountain with its singular bright shade

Like the blue shine on freshly frozen snow,

The after-light upon ice-burdened pines;

Odor of basswood upon a mountain slope,

A scene beloved of bees;

Silence of water above a sunken tree:

The pure serene of memory of one man,—

A ripple widening from a single stone

Winding around the waters of the world.

THEODORE ROETHKE

Can you hear the sighing in the wind? Can you feel the heavy silence in the mountains? Can you sense the restless longing in the sea? Something's coming. . . something better. If the whole inanimate creation is eagerly looking forward to the appearing of Jesus, this same hope — even a brighter hope — should grip your heart and mind.

JONI EARECKSON TADA

A work of art which did not begin in emotion is not art.
PAUL CEZANNE

DEEP CALLS TO DEEP IN THE ROAR OF

YOUR WATERFALLS; ALL YOUR WAVES

AND BREAKERS HAVE SWEPT OVER ME.

PSALM 42:7

LET THE RIVERS CLAP THEIR HANDS, LET

THE MOUNTAINS SING TOGETHER FOR JOY.

PSALM 98:8

God said "Let the land produce vegetation: seed-bearing plants and trees on the land that bear fruit with seed in it, according to their various kinds."

To see a world in a grain of sand and heaven
in a wild flower, hold infinity in the palm
of your hand and eternity in an hour.

WILLIAM BLAKE
Auguries of Innocence

I know for sure that I have an instinct for
color, and that it will come to me more and
more, that painting is in the very marrow
of my bones.

VINCENT VAN GOGH

They'll sell you thousands of greens. Veronese green and emerald green and cadmium green and any sort of green you like; but that particular green, never.

PABLO PICASSO

FLOWERS APPEAR ON THE EARTH;
THE SEASON OF SINGING HAS
COME, THE COOING OF DOVES
IS HEARD IN OUR LAND.

SONG OF SOLOMON 2:12

It must   It must have been your hands

Color has taken hold of me. I don't have to
try to capture it. It will possess me always.
That is the meaning of this happy hour. I
know it. Color and I are one. I am a painter.

PAUL KLEE

MAY GOD GIVE YOU OF HEAVEN'S
DEW AND OF EARTH'S RICHNESS —
AN ABUNDANCE OF GRAIN AND
NEW WINE.

GENESIS 27:28

Colors of nature placed on pallets of land
Fuchsia and tanzanite crafted by hand,
You blinked in the morning and the earth was laid down
You painted the landscapes in siennas and browns.

Flowers and trees grew where nothing had been
Marigolds and daisies were tossed by the wind,
Arrangements of brilliance that spill over the hills
They dine on the dew and the sun's chlorophyll.

You saw the whole picture, dreamt its beauty and grace
A smile of great pleasure must have been on Your face,
"It is good!" You shouted till the rocks thundered down
"It is good!" Still You cry when your artistry is found.

KATHY VICK

THEN THE TREES OF THE FOREST
WILL SING, THEY WILL SING FOR
JOY BEFORE THE LORD, FOR HE
COMES TO JUDGE THE EARTH.

1 CHRONICLES 16:33

The Fourth Day…

God said, "Let there be lights in the expanse of the sky. And let them serve as signs to mark seasons and days and years. . . ."

To explain away the mystery of a great painting — if such a feat were possible — would be irreparable harm. . . . If there is no mystery then there is no "poetry."

GEORGES BRAQUE

Yet he has not left himself without testimony: He has shown
kindness by giving you rain from heaven and crops in their seasons;
he provides you with plenty of food and fills your hearts with joy.

ACTS 14:17

The moon marks off the
seasons, and the sun knows
when to go down.

PSALM 104:19

God made two great lights.

LIGHT IS SWEET, AND IT PLEASES THE EYE TO SEE THE SUN.

ECCLESIASTES 11:7

HE IS LIKE THE LIGHT OF MORNING AT SUNRISE ON A CLOUDLESS

MORNING, LIKE THE BRIGHTNESS AFTER RAIN THAT BRINGS THE

GRASS FROM THE EARTH.

2 SAMUEL 23:4

You saw the universe when it was cold, void and bare

Did You smile when you hung the sun, in the air?

Did sweet words of awe escape on Your tongue?

When You first saw the beauty that You had begun?

Were You like an artist who gets lost in his craft?

Did You stop in the middle, did mistakes make You laugh?

Did Your breath, come like waves when You sketched in the moon?

Were You finished by nightfall, did the moon leave too soon?

God, You gave us our morning, You crafted the night,

You painted them both with a soft, fragile light,

I've seen all the colors that You laid in the sky

Bright ribbons of heaven that make poets sigh.

Tell me, did You know how amazed we would be

When Your purples and oranges ran into the sea?

Did You know we might cry when we saw a sunrise?

You'd revealed who You are in our own artists' eyes?

KATHY VICK

HE REVEALS THE DEEP THINGS
OF DARKNESS AND BRINGS DEEP
SHADOWS INTO THE LIGHT.

JOB 12:22

He also made the stars.

Midnight heavens lit so bright
You paint the sky with stars and light,
Stars whirl and twirl suspended with care
Hand strokes of passion on a canvas of air.

God, You painted the horizons in sapphire hue
With bold strokes of indigo and Mediterranean blue,
You named the hours in the day and the night
Hand brushed Your drama with luminous light.

God, You laid down colors that gave mystery to night
Gave children their dreams, gave the artists their sight,
You blink and the stars all call out Your name
They shimmer and shake, they dance and proclaim.

Sometimes they're like pins pricks of twinkling light
As they chant out Your promises in the black of the night,
God, You gave them rhythm as You paced out the sky
In that velvety liquid where You taught them to fly.

Kathy Vick

I run the tundra of my dreams, I howl to the

stars of my imagination. I fly on the breeze

of my mind and I pour my soul into my

pencil. I dream in color, and see the world

through a rainbow.

Angela
8th grade

WHEN I CONSIDER YOUR HEAVENS, THE WORK
OF YOUR FINGERS, THE MOON AND THE STARS,
WHICH YOU HAVE SET IN PLACE, WHAT IS MAN
THAT YOU ARE MINDFUL OF HIM, THE SON OF
MAN THAT YOU CARE FOR HIM?

PSALM 8:3,4

IT IS I WHO MADE THE EARTH AND CREATED
MANKIND UPON IT. MY OWN HANDS STRETCHED
OUT THE HEAVENS; I MARSHALED THEIR STARRY
HOSTS.

ISAIAH 45:12

*If we are to even attempt to communicate good in our art we
must push out beyond our bent understanding of it and draw from
the depths of God's character.*

NED BUSTARD
It was Good . . . Making Art to the Glory of God

Pour forth
Pour forth

The heavens declare the glory of God; the skies proclaim the work of his hands. Day after day they pour forth speech; night after night they display knowledge. There is no speech or language where their voice is not heard. Their voice goes out into all the earth, their words to the ends of the world.

Psalm 19:1-4

Praise him, sun and moon, praise him, all you shining stars.

Psalm 148:3

IT WAS YOU WHO SET ALL THE

BOUNDARIES OF THE EARTH; YOU

MADE BOTH SUMMER AND WINTER.

PSALM 74:14

And everything that's new has bravely surfaced

Teaching us to breathe

What was frozen through is newly purposed

Turning all things green

So it is with You

And how You make me new

With every season's change

And so it will be

As You are re-creating me

Summer, autumn, winter, spring

NICHOLE NORDEMAN

Every Season

The FIFTH DAY...

So God created the great creatures of the sea and every living and moving thing with which the water teems.

How many are your works, O LORD! In wisdom you made them all; the earth is full of your creatures. There is the sea, vast and spacious, teeming with creatures beyond number — living things both large and small.

Psalm 104:24-25

God created every winged bird according to its kind.

In some mysterious way, the flowers and plants, animals, seascapes and landscapes wait in eager expectation . . . all creation is hoping . . . for a glory yet to be revealed. The apostle Paul tells a little more about this anticipation: "The world of creation cannot as yet see reality, not because it chooses to be blind, but because in God's purpose it has been so limited — yet it has been given hope. And the hope is that in the end the whole of created life will be rescued from the tyranny of change and decay, and have its share in that magnificent liberty which can only belong to the children of God!" (Romans 8:20, 21 Phillips).

JONI EARECKSON TADA

Don't paint bit by bit, but paint everything at once by placing tones everywhere, with brushstrokes of the right color and value, while noticing what is alongside.

CAMILLE PISSARO

God blessed them and said, "Be fruitful and increase in number and fill the water in the seas, and let the birds increase on the earth."

PRAISE THE LORD FROM
THE EARTH, YOU GREAT
SEA CREATURES AND ALL
OCEAN DEPTHS.

PSALM 148:7

The Sixth Day...

God said, "Let the land produce livestock, creatures that move along the ground, and wild animals, each according to its kind."

The job of the artist is always to deepen the mystery.

FRANCIS BACON

But ask the animals, and they
will teach you, or the birds of
the air, and they will tell you;
or speak to the earth, and it
will teach you, or let the fish
of the sea inform you. Which of
all these does not know that
the hand of the LORD has done
this? In his hand is the life
of every creature and the
breath of all mankind.

JOB 12:7-10

For every animal of the forest is mine, and the

cattle on a thousand hills.

Psalm 50:10

God said, "I give you every seed-bearing plant... and every tree that has fruit with seed in it."

When we practice our art as servants to the work, whether the work is successful or not becomes secondary to the work God will be doing in us through that art.

JANICE ELSHEIMER
The Creative Call

The true work of art is but a shadow of
the divine perfection.

MICHELANGELO

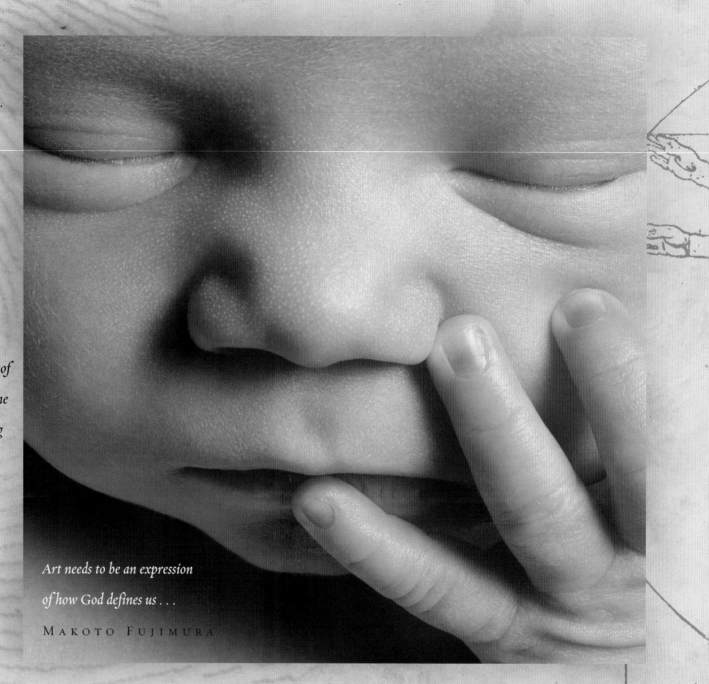

God created man
in His own image.

God's goodness is evident in
so many areas: the very gift of
life, the offer of salvation, the
provision of deep and lasting
relationships, the ability to
create art, and a beautiful
world to inhabit, not to
mention our daily bread.

NED BUSTARD
*It was Good . . . Making Art to
the Glory of God*

*Art needs to be an expression
of how God defines us . . .*

MAKOTO FUJIMURA

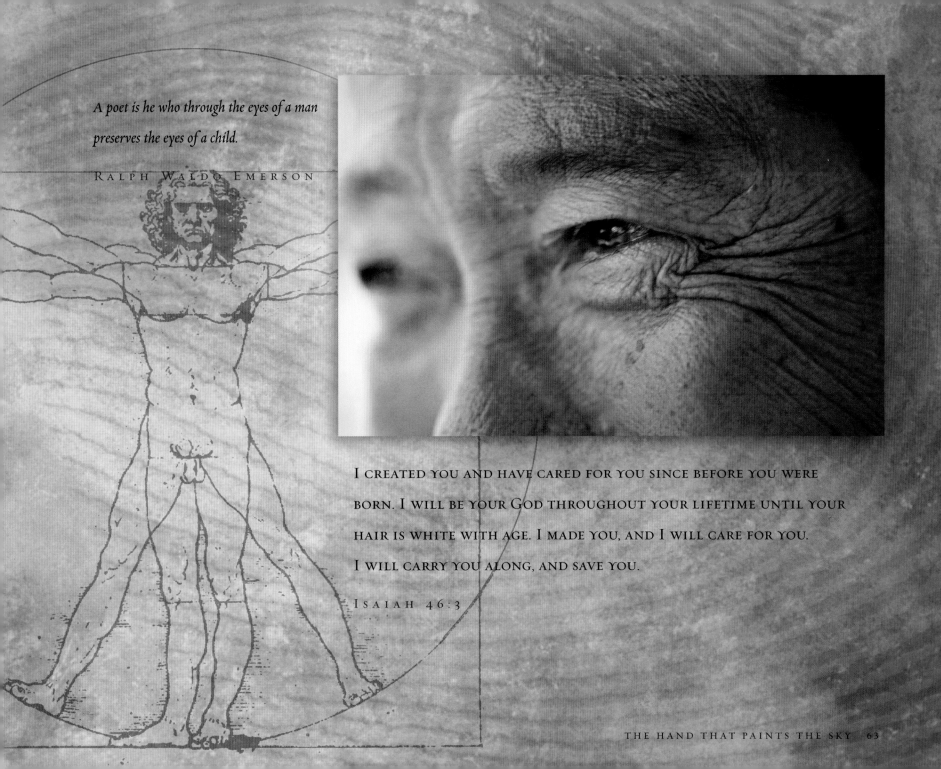

A poet is he who through the eyes of a man preserves the eyes of a child.

RALPH WALDO EMERSON

I CREATED YOU AND HAVE CARED FOR YOU SINCE BEFORE YOU WERE

BORN. I WILL BE YOUR GOD THROUGHOUT YOUR LIFETIME UNTIL YOUR

HAIR IS WHITE WITH AGE. I MADE YOU, AND I WILL CARE FOR YOU.

I WILL CARRY YOU ALONG, AND SAVE YOU.

ISAIAH 46:3

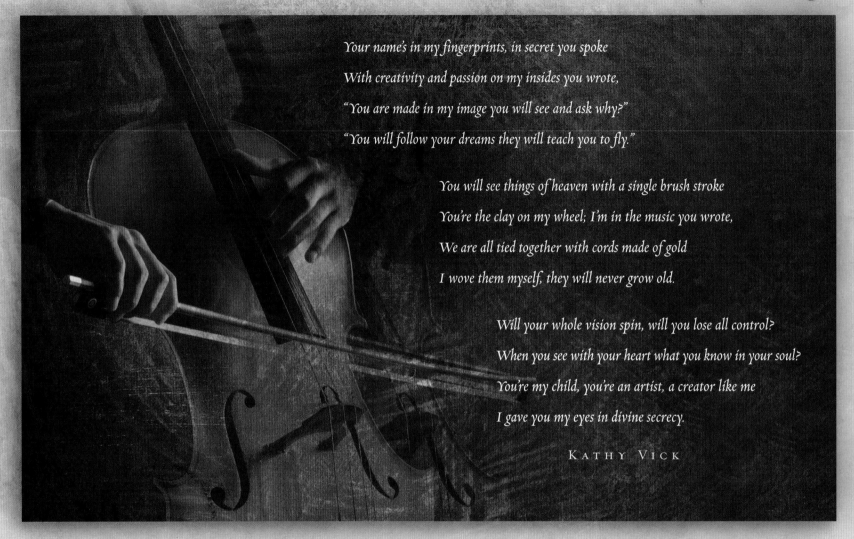

Your name's in my fingerprints, in secret you spoke

With creativity and passion on my insides you wrote,

"You are made in my image you will see and ask why?"

"You will follow your dreams they will teach you to fly."

You will see things of heaven with a single brush stroke

You're the clay on my wheel; I'm in the music you wrote,

We are all tied together with cords made of gold

I wove them myself, they will never grow old.

Will your whole vision spin, will you lose all control?

When you see with your heart what you know in your soul?

You're my child, you're an artist, a creator like me

I gave you my eyes in divine secrecy.

KATHY VICK

His image is woven into the fabric of everything we are. His thumbprint on our lives affects us in ways we will never even begin to understand.

His divine beauty, which is part of our essence as well, demands a response.

MICHAEL CARD *Scribbling in the Sand*

He has made everything beautiful in its time. He has also set eternity in the hearts of men; yet they cannot fathom what God has done from beginning to end.

ECCLESIASTES 3:11

I paint a portrait of you

Thus the heavens
and the earth
were completed
in all their vast
array.

God saw all that
He had made,
and it was very
good.

Taking captive the human mind and heart
involves more than fear or facts, emotion or
knowledge. . . God is out to recapture all that
we are or can hope to be. Not just the mind
or the heart but the mind of the heart, the
heart of the mind, which is the imagination.

MICHAEL CARD
Scribbling in the Sand

"Creating," is not merely restricted to the
"arts" as we call it, but extends through all
dimensions of our life; it penetrates our
moral sphere. What we say, how we live,
these are all sourced in creative choices.
Van Gogh, the great, penniless artist wrote:
"The more I think it over, the more I feel
that there is nothing more truly artistic
than to love people."

PATRICK ENDRES

I search the landscape with the hope of capturing part of nature's beauty. From early morning to late evening, overcast to sunny, each situation is unique and has its own personality/feeling. I attempt to bring the viewer into my work with strong foregrounds or leading lines to entice the eyes to be drawn further into the scene. With correct light, composition and exposure I might capture that moment that may only happen once in a lifetime.

STEVE TERRILL

The SEVENTH DAY...

I am the Alpha and the Omega, the First and the Last,
the Beginning and the End.

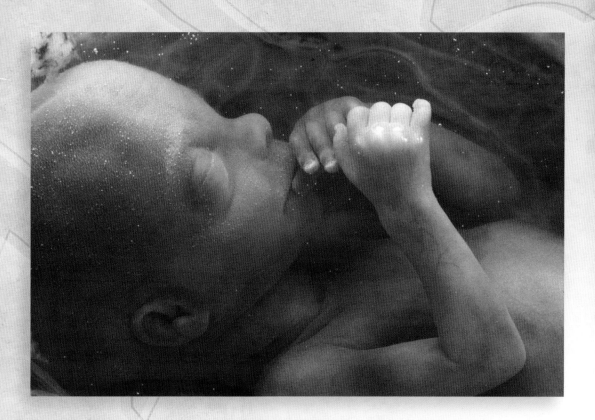

You built a bridge

That reached from heaven down to me

Though I'm unworthy

Once a captive now I'm free

Breathe life, oh breathe life into me

And let Your fire consume me

CINDY MORGAN

& CHRIS RODRIGUEZ

God rested from all His work. And God blessed the seventh day and made it holy, because on it He rested from all the work of creating that He had done.

Shall what is formed say to him who formed it, "He did not make me"? Can the pot say of the potter, "He knows nothing"?

ISAIAH 29:16

An Afterthought...

I have always loved Genesis and the incredible language of intimacy that God used to describe each scene. The words are like music: "The earth was formless and empty and darkness was hovering over the face of the deep and the Spirit of God was hovering over the waters." And: "Let there be light . . . and the expanse he called sky . . . and there was evening and there was morning. The first day" (Genesis 1).

But why, after creating such perfection and beauty in each plant and animal — creatures whose single purpose of existence is to glorify Him — would He think of *us*? We who would rebel, doubt and disappoint?

After He saw all that He created and its breathtaking magnificence, perhaps even the almighty Himself could scarcely contain His joy. Perhaps He desired to share it with those He would call His children. Parents have no greater joy than to see the wonder of something they, too, once marveled at, made new again through the eyes of their child: the first snowfall, a lightning storm, a spectacular rising or setting of the sun. This sharing of joy is one of the few pleasures in life that feels complete, undiluted and pure.

For me, it has never been in a mighty cathedral or a country church where I have felt God the most. Not in a museum containing great works of art or even in the triumphant sounds of Handel's *Messiah*. For me, it has been in the small moments — a bird lighting on the rock of a trickling creek, a flock of wild geese flying overhead, or a slow, steady sunset that you cannot look away from for fear that there will never be another quite so beautiful.

The bittersweet is that such scenes remain for only a breath — then vanish forever. That's what makes a photograph so priceless. A moment of the Creator's artistry that may have disappeared forever gets captured in the instant it occurred. And ever afterward we can see it and remember the feeling of power and awe that it brought us in that long-ago moment.

So I say, thank you Father, that You made all of these visions for us, Your children. Thank You for giving the rich and the poor the same eyes to gaze upon the beauty You have laid before us, the great reach of Your mercy and love that never speaks louder than in the quiet moments when we behold what You have created and breathe in the life that You gave us.

CINDY MORGAN

PHOTO CREDITS

STEVE TERRILL PHOTOGRAPHY, *www.terrillphoto.com*, cover, pages 3, 8
(lower right), 14, 18-21, 24-30, 32(upper left), 33-35, 37-38, 40-41,
59(lower left), 61, 65, 67, 72

PATRICK J. ENDRES, *www.alaskaphotographics.com*, pages 6-7, 12, 16-17, 36, 42,
46-47, 48-49, 56, 59(center), 60(lower right), 64(lower right), 66

CORBIS, *www.corbis.com*, pages 4, 45

GETTY, *www.gettyimages.com*, pages 50-51, 54, 60, 62-63, 65

IMAGE BANK, *www.imagebank.com*, page 69

NATIONAL GEOGRAPHIC, *www.ngs.com*, pages 54(upper left), 59(upper right)

all others taken from the following photo CD's:
ARTVILLE: *Impressionist Backgrounds, Nature's Backgrounds, Wings in Detail*

CORBIS: *Visions of Nature*

DIGITAL STOCK: *Animals in Action, Backgrounds from Nature, Conceptual Backgrounds,
Flowers, Four Seasons, Nature & Landscape, Stormchaser*

IMAGE CLUB GRAPHICS: *Circa Art--Antique Maps & Charts, Circa Art—Impressionists*

PHOTODISC: *Sea Life, Spacescapes*

Brushstroked photos by ANNELI HOLMGREN

EDITIORIAL CREDITS:

Scribbling in the Sand, written by Michael Card, *Intervarsity Press*,
Downers Grove, IL, copyright 2002

It Was Good: Making Art to the Glory of God, Editor: Ned Bustard,
Square Halo Books, Baltimore, MD, copyright 2000

The Creative Call, written by Janice Elsheimer, *Waterbrook Press/Shaw Books*,
Colorado Springs, CO, copyright 2001

Rainbows for A Fallen World, written by Calvin Seerveld, *Toronto
Tuppence Press*, Toronto, Ontario, copyright 1980

The Genesee Diary: Report from a Trappist Monastery, written by
Henri J.M. Nouwen, *Image Books*, reissued edition 1981

The Art of the Soul: Meditations for the Creative Spirit, written by
Joy Sawyer, *Broadman & Holman Publishers*, Nashville, TN, copyright 2000

Breathe life oh breathe life into

You paint the morning

With the motion of Your hand

You move the water

make an ocean from dry land

Everything that lives in heaven

And on earth

You have created from

The dawn of every birth

Breathing life

Breathing life

Breathing life

Breathing life